Cuyahoga Valley
National Recreation Area

Published by
Cuyahoga Valley Association
in cooperation with National Park Service at Cuyahoga Valley National Recreation Area

This Project Was Made Possible Due To A Grant From

The George Gund Foundation
Cleveland, Ohio

Cuyahoga Valley Association · P.O. Box 222 · Peninsula, Ohio 44264 · 330-657-2909
E-mail: CVA@bright.net · Web Site: http://www.nps.gov/cuva/cva
Editor in Chief - Kevin O'Neil
Associate Editor - Susan Kosich · Text by Diane Chalfant · Art Direction - Jerry Moody · Copy Editor - Bruce Winges
Photography Editors: Diane Chalfant, Kevin O'Neil and Jerry Moody
Printed at Oliver Printing - Twinsburg, Ohio
ISBN 0-9633845-1-1

The story of the Cuyahoga Valley is the story of moving water. Moving water defines Cuyahoga Valley National Recreation Area today, as it did before the time of the Ohio & Erie Canal, before the time of the Cuyahoga River, before the time of the glaciers. Moving water was the primary force that first created and then exposed the park's ancient sandstone ledges and it is moving water that continually redefines the Cuyahoga Valley today.

First, it was the flow of fine-grained sediments into a giant, shallow inland sea, creating huge, fan-shaped deltas that hardened into our bedrock of sandstones and shales.
Giant armored prehistoric shark-like fish of the Devonian Period hunted in this sand-bottomed sea over 350 million years ago. Millions of years later, fast-moving mountain streams washed quartz pebbles into these seas, creating the beautiful sandstone we know today as Sharon Conglomerate.

It was moving water again—this time in the form of a giant frozen sheet, a mile or more deep, slowly funneling into ancient river valleys like thick, spilled pancake batter -- that chased cool-climate plants such as hemlock and birch southward.

four

At times it paused, dropping its debris—sand, gravel and clay. Today, as we hike the valley and find the occasional smooth rounded large granite boulder, we are pausing where a glacier paused thousands of years ago and dropped its souvenir from Canada.

five

Trapped between the highlands of today's Akron and the edge of the glacier, meltwater formed a giant lake, which covered the southern half of today's Cuyahoga Valley National Recreation Area. As the last glacier retreated north, tributaries of meltwater cut into glacial debris, creating the many ravines of the Cuyahoga Valley.

Within these ravines, streams like Brandywine Creek descend the steep valley walls, creating water-falls as they make their way to the Cuyahoga River. It is at places like Brandywine Falls where moving water reveals the layered geologic past of ancient sea floors, and we see the motion of currents hardened into sandy ripple marks in stone.

eight

Those who attempt to scramble valley slopes know that the loose rocks, sand and dirt are only fill. The accelerated movement of water running off streets, parking lots and denuded property rushing down these unstable slopes robs soil from tree roots, eventually depositing it in the Cuyahoga River. In this, as in many ways, the valley is affected by activities that occur beyond its boundaries. Toppled and sliding trees are a normal part of Cuyahoga's ever-changing landscape.

This is a diverse landscape of river floodplain, steep and gentle valley walls forested by deciduous and evergreen woods, wet ravines and upland plateaus. The variety of plants and animals that live in the valley is truly remarkable, especially considering how close the park is to Cleveland and Akron. This diversity is due to the park's glacial legacy and its location. Situated at the eastern brim of the great prairies, and at the western edge of the Appalachian Highlands, the Cuyahoga Valley is a natural "melting pot"—a place where inhabitants from many different regions live. Its moist, cool ravines are post-glacial oases, supporting a variety of unusual plant species that depend on cooler climates to survive.

Here plants such as wintergreen, Canada mayflower, and trout-lily thrive below a canopy of yellow birch and eastern hemlock. Yet, within a couple of miles, purple coneflowers and bluestem—holdouts from an earlier prairie—bloom in the August sun. On the high ground of the Appalachian ridges and on the higher, dryer ridges of the Cuyahoga Valley, you will find white oaks. They live here with tulip trees, American hornbeam, white ash and hickories. Beech and sugar maples are common throughout the valley.

It is the seasonality, the yellow, orange, and red fall color show punctuated by the bold evergreens, that draws people. Perhaps it is the symbolic marking of the passage of time, as the nearly one hundred tree species go from bare branches to full fall splendor, or perhaps it is the appeal of Indian summer, or nostalgia for an indiscernible pleasantry from some early time, but for whatever reason, autumn draws visitors en masse to the Cuyahoga Valley.

thirteen

What visitor doesn't instinctively slow, driving park roads, peering into the woods or across a field, searching for a glimpse of a white-tailed deer or coyote? These are animals that thrive in the open areas and edges between woodlands and fields. While deer were less abundant when settlers first arrived, the coyote had not yet migrated into Ohio. Like raccoons, skunks and

woodchucks, deer are common today. It was the opening of the forest to agriculture, habitation and other activities that encouraged the development of a richer diversity of wildlife than existed originally. Of the more than 40 species of mammals in the park, some are making surprising comebacks.

The beaver is a prime example of recovery. Arguably the most popular spot for many in Cuyahoga Valley National Recreation Area is the Beaver Marsh. It is one of many beaver-caused impoundments in the park. Fifteen years ago, naming such a place THE Beaver Marsh made sense. After an absence of nearly 150 years, the return of beaver to the Cuyahoga Valley was very significant. There was only one beaver marsh then. The beaver found ideal habitat in the valley, and today, there are dozens of beaver ponds. The Beaver Marsh is the location of a former auto salvage scrap yard. Although people cleaned it up, it was the beaver that made it an inspired place. Today, artists and photographers are almost as common as the frogs, turtles, wood ducks, and fish that flourish here.

In the quiet dusk of the beaver pond, the background lull is interrupted by the sound of moving water. The broad, quarter-mile horseshoe shaped beaver dam isn't entirely water-tight; now the trickle of a leak signals the beavers to resume work and reminds us that moving water will prevail in the Cuyahoga Valley.

At once the most visible and the most elusive of fauna at Cuyahoga Valley National Recreation Area are the birds. Just as the roads on the floor of the valley are secondary to the interstates as travel routes for us, so the valley is located between two major avian migration routes. Nearly 175 transient bird species pass through the valley, and another 100 or so nest here, and about 60 make their year-round living here. Robins, wood thrushes, many species of warblers, eastern phoebe, and tree swallows are common.

While we may regret the disappearance of the vast virgin forests that once covered this region, we can celebrate and enjoy the vistas, pastures, meadows and ponds. These openings in the landscape provide soaring space for the large birds—the red-shouldered and broad-winged hawks, and the turkey vultures. This is the valuable open space that helps define Cuyahoga Valley National Recreation Area. It is the formerly rare wood ducks, blue birds, great blue herons and kingfishers that remind us of the value of wetlands; but biannual migrating warblers remind us that this green oasis is so important as a spot of rest and replenishment for birds as well as humans.

Moving water attracted people to the Cuyahoga Valley. Archeology shows us the same qualities that make a certain park location desirable to develop for recreation today also attracted people over and over again in the past. The adage, "a good place to camp is a good place to camp" is quite true here. We find Woodland period villages along the same river floodplain terrace as 19th century hamlets.

Small settlements with historic homes and barns dot the valley. It is the rich soils of the valley floor, periodically replenished by river flooding, that drew people to the Cuyahoga Valley for farming. Today, the corn and pumpkin farms and historic barns remind us of the small family farm lifestyle of times past.

Over time, the Cuyahoga River has served many functions. It provided a livelihood, a transportation route, food source, replenishment for the Ohio & Erie Canal, the power for grist mills, a source of electricity, and unfortunately, for more than 100 years, an open sewer. Today the Cuyahoga River is the story of reclamation and renewal in process.

Like the river, the Ohio & Erie Canal is often described as the centerpiece of Cuyahoga Valley National Recreation Area. Today as one looks at the nearly perfect, dappled reflection of the tree-lined banks of the Towpath in the watered section of the canal, or more likely examines the dry and sometimes overgrown sandstone ruins of canal locks and culverts, it is difficult to imagine the activity surrounding the canal during its heyday. Built to open the interior of Ohio to the Great Lakes, to the Ohio River and trade, the canal was instrumental to the development of the commercial and economic life of Ohio a century and a half ago. The first link of the canal opened in the valley in 1827 providing water access to Lake Erie.

By 1832 farmers in the interior of Ohio could get their crops to eastern markets. For 50 years the Ohio & Erie Canal dominated the north-south transportation route in the Cuyahoga Valley. Ironically, it was moving water—the great flood of 1913, that sealed the fate of the canal. Today, in many places, the canal prism has filled in, leaving the canal an unrecognizable secret given away only by the presence of the Towpath Trail.

The sound of the Cuyahoga Valley Scenic Railroad whistle is as much a part of the Cuyahoga Valley today as it was 100 years ago. A rail route to the Cuyahoga Valley was completed in 1880. The "Valley Railroad" paralleled the Cuyahoga River and the Ohio & Erie Canal. Railroad stations were built throughout the valley, providing passenger service and linking cross-roads towns to Cleveland, Akron, and Canton. Today, the train once again provides visitors a link between the Cuyahoga Valley and the cities.

In the evening when the train whistle is silent, when the Towpath is dark and quiet, the waterfalls of the park continue to respond to the force of gravity agelessly, unaffected by the ebb and flow of daily human activity. They flow constantly night and day, throughout the seasons, throughout the decades, existing in stark contrast to the urgency of the business that whizzes people by at 65 mph just a few hundred yards away on the interstates.

Often, when the sun is shining clear in the early morning around the Cuyahoga Valley, something entirely different is happening within. The park's signature, a misty fog, sits heavily in the valley. It seeks the lowest areas, spreading its ethereal fingers into the ravines, placing a quiet spell on the valley. As we drive Route 303, descending into the valley, we become cautious and are forced to slow. We look for the shadow of something—a deer?

It is water, now on crisp winter mornings, that covers the remaining leaves on the trees with hoarfrost, long after the uplands have warmed and melted away to reveal the normal landscape. The protected, cool microclimate of the valley holds the magical crystals until the sun hits the valley floor.

Ironically, it is the rush of tens of thousands of gallons of water, cascading over Brandywine Falls and other falls within the Cuyahoga Valley, that draws people to slow down, pause, appreciate and reflect in Cuyahoga Valley National Recreation Area.

thirty two

thirty three

Early winter and late spring floods seem powerful enough—sometimes causing valley residents to leave their homes for a day or two until water subsides. Flooding cuts and erodes the river banks, sometimes threatening homes, trails, railroad tracks and roads. We have endless skirmishes with the river, adding rock gabions and riprap, attempting to keep it within the confines of its former course. While dramatic to us, these events are only the small games of a small river, jumping its bank, shortcutting its curves, all played out within the arena of a much larger river valley confine. In the end, of course, the river will triumph.

Cuyahoga Valley National Recreation Area's beauty is subtle. Unlike national parks in the west, it doesn't boast superlatives—no deepest canyons, tallest trees; no geothermal features or mountains. Yet, like the largest of the national parks, there are over three million visits annually. Why? The answer is that the Cuyahoga Valley has a cumulative effect on its visitors, the kind that draws one back, again and again, each time giving more depth, meaning and psychological investment. It is a layered park, a place that can only be fully understood after multiple visits. Cuyahoga Valley National Recreation Area has a rolling, quiet beauty, yet a kind of overwhelming effect; the kind that makes visitors want to stay and residents deeply protective. Today, its value as a vestige of something that no longer exists becomes more and more profound each year, as development surrounds and pressures the park.

thirty nine

The force that created Cuyahoga Valley National Recreation Area is moving water. Water shapes and changes the valley on its own schedule, sometimes dramatically with floods, but more often slowly, imperceptibly, one drop of rain at a time.

Our time in the valley is just a still frame in an epic-length film of geologic drama with acts including the appearance and disappearance of seas, mountains, and mile-high glaciers. We have been visitors and residents to this valley for a very, very brief time, yet we have affected it dramatically.

One needs only to stand in the center of the park and look to the sky. The omniscient interstates bisect the park north and south, barely touching yet dramatically influencing the park, symbols of the accelerated pace in which the park itself stands in stark contrast.

We are reminded that Cuyahoga Valley National Recreation Area is vulnerable and precious, and quite, quite finite.

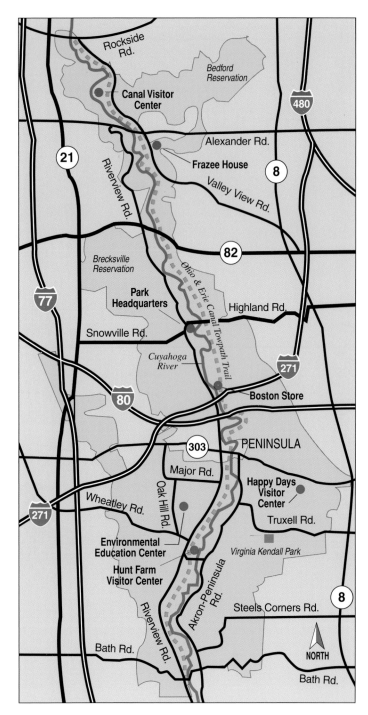

For more information about Cuyahoga Valley National Recreation Area, contact:
Superintendent
Cuyahoga Valley NRA
15610 Vaughn Road
Brecksville, Ohio 44141
800-433-1986
http://www.nps.gov/cuva/home.htm

Photo Credits:
- Adams, Ian - 30
- Buescher, Jim - 5, 9, 16T
- Buescher, Paul - 15L, 26B
- Cawley, Tom (NPS) - 23B
- Dvorak, Dave - 4, 29B
- Good, Michael F. - Cover, 36, 37T
- Jones, Tom - 12B, 14B, 20B, 33, 42T, 42L
- Ketchum, Robert Glenn - 1, 3T, 22, 38
- Muench, David - 17
- Neill, William - 40
- O'Hara, Pat - 39T
- O'Neil, Kevin C. - 2, 3B, 6B, 10, 13, 20T, 21B, 23T, 24, 25LR, 27, 31, 32, 37B, 39B, 41, 44, Back Cover
- Roetzel, Jim - 11B, 14T, 15T, 15R, 16B, 18, 19T, 19R, 26T, 29T
- Rowell, Galen - 28
- Saus, Ed - 8, 21T
- Shaw, John - 11T
- Stimac, Carl - 12T
- Thomas, Tim - 25T, 34
- Wilson, Peter - 35, 42R
- Winges, Bruce - 19L
- Witt, Michael - 6T, 7
- Wolfe, Art - 43

Special thanks for donating the use of all images:
O'Neil, Kevin C.

Special thanks for donating use of images at a discount:
Good, Michael F.
Roetzel, Jim

Legend:
T- Top, B- Bottom, L-Left, R-Right

Boston Store, c.1996